Keto Diet

on a Budget

Quick, Simple and Cheap Low-Carb Recipes for Beginners on Ketogenic Diet

Celine Cunningham

Table of Contents

Introduction

What is Keto Diet?

Keto diet (Ketogenic diet) this is a low-carb diet with a high percentage of fat in the diet, in which the body produces ketones in the liver and uses them as energy.

Initially the main most familiar and accessible source of energy for our body is glucose. When you eat something high in carbohydrates, our body processes them into glucose, which increases the blood sugar and for its stabilization and the distribution of glucose in the cells of the body, the pancreas produces insulin.

Glucose is the simplest molecule in our body that is converted and used as energy, so it will be chosen over any other source of energy.

Insulin is produced to process glucose in the blood by moving it throughout the body.

Since glucose is used as an energy source, your fats are not needed and therefore accumulate. Typically, in a normal, higher carbohydrate diet, the body will use glucose as the main form of energy. By reducing carbohydrate intake, the body is induced into a condition known as ketosis.

Ketosis is a natural condition of our body, which starts with a low content of glucose in the diet. With him, the body produces ketones, splitting fatty acids, to provide us with a sufficient level of energy, nutrition of brain cells and organs.

The main goal and ultimate goal of keto diets is to switch us to the state of ketosis. It is important to understand that it does not start with a lowcalorie

intake, but with a low carbohydrate content in the diet.

Our bodies are incredibly adaptive - as soon as they lack glucose, they easily switch to ketosis and begin to use fats as the main source of energy.

The optimal level of ketones and low blood sugar levels give us a lot of advantages: from a general improvement in health and a decrease in the percentage of subcutaneous fat, to an increase in mental concentration, energy level and vitality.

A keto-diet implies a high fat content, a moderate protein content and a very low carbohydrate content.

Nutrient intake should be about 70% fat, 25% protein and 5% carbohydrates.

What Keto Can Do For You

Keto has its origins in treating healthcare conditions such as epilepsy, type 2

diabetes, cardiovascular disease, metabolic syndrome, auto-brewery

syndrome and high blood pressure but now has much wider application in

weight control.

This diet, then, will take you above and beyond typical results and propel

youinto a new realm of total body health. If you want to look and feel the

best youpossibly can, all without sacrificing your love of delicious food, then

this is thecookbook for you.

Why are people going on the ketogenic diet even if they don't have

epilepsy? As the keto diet became a more popular alternative to fasting,

people began noticing additional benefits, like weight loss. Here are the

most reported benefits of the low-carb, high-fat diet:

Cutting out lots of carbs can lead to weight loss

Significantly restricting carbs causes the body to produce ketones, but it also

prevents excess glucose from getting stored as body fat. Lots of people who

go on the keto diet find that losing weight is much easier. This is especially

true if your current diet is high in refined, simple carbs like white bread,

pasta, and sugar. Carbs are not inherently evil - as we mentioned before,

the body actually needs them - but refined carbs are not very nutritious and

usually end up stored as fat. When you eliminate them, weight loss is more

likely.

The diet improves energy levels

You probably are familiar with the sluggish feeling after eating a carb-heavy meal. That's because your body is working so hard to process the carbs. You get an initial burst of energy and then a crash. When you cut out those refined carbs and instead eat foods higher in fat, that fatigue goes away. Your blood sugar levels become more stabilized throughout the day instead of going on a rollercoaster. The high-fat diet also helps with mental energy, since the brain is especially fond of fats found in coconut oil and fatty fish.

Your skin and hair health improve

A lot of people who go on the keto diet report having healthier skin, hair, and even fingernails. Fat is a hydrating nutrient, and hair and skin love it. Hair becomes shinier, sleeker, and less brittle. Skin also becomes healthier and less dry, while cutting out inflammatory foods like sugar can help clear up acne.

The keto diet might prevent certain diseases

There isn't a ton of research into the keto diet's effect on disease, but early studies are intriguing. Heart disease is a top killer, especially in the United States, and the keto diet can help people maintain better blood pressure. A high body mass is linked to heart disease, so losing weight thanks to the keto diet can also protect a person from the disease. The keto diet's effect on the brain is also significant, and studies have shown that ketones might help prevent and even treat brain disorders like Alzheimer's.

The Keto Flu and how to avoid it.

Keto flu is not a virus that infects only those who decide to try a ketogenic diet. This is the body's response to carbohydrate restriction.

The most common symptoms of keto-flu are craving for sugar, dizziness, irritability, fog in the head and poor concentration, stomach pain, nausea, cramps, muscle soreness and insomnia.

To avoid this, follow these simple rules:

1. Drink more water (with a pinch of unrefined salt).

Hydration is vital, especially when you are on a ketogenic diet. If during a keto diet you do not drink enough water, you can easily dehydrate and experience side effects.

2. Supplement your diet with sodium, potassium and magnesium.

To get enough potassium, add avocados and leafy greens such as spinach to your diet. Add a little crude salt to each meal and to water to replenish sodium levels.

Magnesium is another important mineral that can significantly ease your transition to ketosis. Although you do not lose magnesium, while limiting carbohydrates, it is important to help you prevent and eliminate cramps, improve sleep quality and increase insulin sensitivity. Simply add pumpkin seeds, almonds and spinach to your diet.

3. Eat more fat.

To help your body adapt, eat more fat. Fat provides Acetyl-CoA liver

cells, which they can use to make ketones.

4. In the morning, do exercises with low intensity.

When you wake up, fill the bottle with water and a pinch of salt, and go for

a walk. The walk should be at a pace where you can easily talk without

gasping. It is desirable to walk about an hour.

As you continue walking, you should feel better and better and more and

more awake. This is a form of low intensity exercise that will help increase

fat burning, and you will not have to suffer from keto flu.

5. Relieve stress through meditation.

When you start a ketogenic diet, you may be tenser and more irritable

than usual. This is due to the fact that your cortisol levels are slightly

higher than usual.

To help reduce cortisol levels and improve overall well-being, it is best to

do daily meditation.

Every day, for 15 minutes, just sit silently, inhaling and exhaling slowly

and deeply.

The purpose of meditation is not to be thoughtless, so as not to be

distracted by the thought, but to concentrate on breathing. This is how you train your mind so that life is less stressful.

6. A good sleep is the key to success.

Another way to reduce stress levels is to ensure good sleep. Good sleep

is especially important for ketogenic diets. Without this, cortisol levels

will increase, which complicates keto-flu and keto-adaptation. Sleep at

least 7-9 hours every night, and if you feel tired in the middle of the day,

lie down for 30 minutes or meditate.

To fall asleep faster at night, turn off all lights (including the phone) at

least 30 minutes before you go to bed. This will help you translate your

mind from work mode to sleep mode.

Breakfast Recipes

1. Shrimp And Bacon Breakfast

Preparation time: 10 minutes **Cooking time:** 15 minutes **Servings:** 4

Ingredients:

- 1 cup mushrooms, sliced
- 4 bacon slices, chopped
- 4 ounces smoked salmon, chopped
- 4 ounces shrimp, deveined
- Salt and black pepper to the taste
- ½ cup coconut cream

Instructions:

1. Heat up a pan over medium heat, add bacon, stir and cook for 5 minutes.

2. Add mushrooms, stir and cook for 5 minutes more.

3. Add salmon, stir and cook for 3 minutes.

4. Add shrimp and cook for 2 minutes.

5. Add salt, pepper and coconut cream, stir, cook for 1 minute, take off heat and divide between plates.

Nutrition: cal.340, fat 23, fiber 1, carbs 4, protein 17

2. <u>Delicious Mexican Breakfast</u>

Preparation time: 10 minutes **Cooking time:** 30 minutes **Servings:** 8

Ingredients: ½ cup enchilada sauce

- 1 pound pork, ground
- 1 pound chorizo, chopped
- Salt and black pepper to the taste
- 8 eggs
- 1 tomato, chopped
- 3 tbsp. ghee
- ½ cup red onion, chopped
- 1 avocado, pitted, peeled and chopped

14

Instructions:

1. In a bowl, mix pork with chorizo, stir and spread on a lined baking form.

2. Spread enchilada sauce on top, introduce in the oven at 350 degrees F and bake for 20 minutes.

3. Heat up a pan with the ghee over medium heat, add eggs and scramble them well.

4. Take pork mix out of the oven and spread scrambled eggs over them.

5. Sprinkle salt, pepper, tomato, onion and avocado, divide between plates and serve.

Nutrition: cal.400, fat 32, fiber 4, carbs 7, protein 25

3. <u>Breakfast Pie</u>

Preparation time: 10 minutes **Cooking time:** 45 minutes **Servings:** 8

Ingredients:

- ½ onion, chopped
- 1 pie crust
- ½ red bell pepper, chopped
- ¾ pound beef, ground
- Salt and black pepper to the taste
- 3 tbsp. taco seasoning
- A handful cilantro, chopped
- 8 eggs
- 1 tsp. coconut oil
- 1 tsp. baking soda
- Mango salsa for serving

Instructions:

1. Heat up a pan with the oil over medium heat, add beef, cook

until it browns and mixes with salt, pepper and taco seasoning.

2. Stir again, transfer to a bowl and leave aside for now.

3. Heat up the pan again over medium heat with cooking juices

from the meat, add onion and bell pepper, stir and cook for 4

minutes.

16

4. Add eggs, baking soda and some salt and stir well.

5. Add cilantro, stir again and take off heat.

6. Spread beef mix in pie crust, add veggies mix and spread over meat, introduce in the oven at 350 degrees F and bake for 45 minutes.

7. Leave the pie to cool down a bit, slice, divide between plates and serve with mango salsa on top.

Nutrition: cal.198, fat 11, fiber 1, carbs 12, protein 12

4. Breakfast Stir Fry

Preparation time: 10 minutes **Cooking time:** 30 minutes **Servings:** 2

Ingredients:

- ½ pounds beef meat, minced
- 2 tsp. red chili flakes
- 1 tbsp. tamari sauce
- 2 bell peppers, chopped
- 1 tsp. chili powder
- 1 tbsp. coconut oil
- Salt and black pepper to the taste

For the bok choy:

- 6 bunches bok choy, trimmed and chopped
- 1 tsp. ginger, grated
- Salt to the taste
- 1 tbsp. coconut oil

For the eggs:

- 1 tbsp. coconut oil
- 2 eggs

Instructions:

1. Heat up a pan with 1 tbsp. coconut oil over medium high heat, add beef and bell peppers, stir and cook for 10 minutes.

2. Add salt, pepper, tamari sauce, chili flakes and chili powder, stir, cook for 4 minutes more and take off heat.

3. Heat up another pan with 1 tbsp. oil over medium heat, add bok choy, stir and cook for 3 minutes.

4. Add salt and ginger, stir, cook for 2 minutes more and take off heat.

5. Heat up the third pan with 1 tbsp. oil over medium heat, crack eggs and fry them.

6. Divide beef and bell peppers mix into 2 bowls.

Nutrition: cal.248, fat 14, fiber 4, carbs 10, protein 14

5. Delicious Breakfast Skillet

Preparation time: 10 minutes **Cooking time:** 30 minutes **Servings:** 4

Ingredients:

- 8 ounces mushrooms, chopped
- Salt and black pepper to the taste
- 1 pound pork, minced
- 1 tbsp. coconut oil
- ½ tsp. garlic powder
- ½ tsp. basil, dried
- 2 tbsp. Dijon mustard
- 2 zucchinis, chopped

Instructions:

1. Heat up a pan with the oil over medium high heat, add mushrooms, stir and cook for 4 minutes.

2. Add zucchinis, salt and pepper, stir and cook for 4 minutes more.

3. Add pork, garlic powder, basil, more salt and pepper, stir and cook until meat is done.

4. Add mustard, stir, cook for 3 minutes more, divide into bowls and serve.

Nutrition: cal.240, fat 15, fiber 2, carbs 9, protein 17

6. <u>Breakfast Casserole</u>

Preparation time: 10 minutes **Cooking time:** 40 minutes **Servings:** 4

Ingredients:

- 10 eggs
- 1 pound pork sausage, chopped
- 1 yellow onion, chopped
- 3 cups spinach, torn
- Salt and black pepper to the taste
- 3 tbsp. avocado oil

Instructions:

1. Heat up a pan with 1 tbsp. oil over medium heat, add

sausage, stir and brown it for 4 minutes.

2. Add onion, stir and cook for 3 minutes more.

3. Add spinach, stir and cook for 1 minute.

4. Grease a baking dish with the rest of the oil and spread sausage

mix.

5. Whisk eggs and add them to sausage mix.

6. Stir gently, introduce in the oven at 350 degrees F and bake for

30 minutes.

7. Leave casserole to cool down for a few minutes before serving

it for breakfast.

Nutrition: cal.345, fat 12, fiber 1, carbs 8, protein 22

Main & Lunch Recipes

7. <u>Simple Asparagus Lunch</u>

Preparation time: 10 minutes **Cooking time:** 10 minutes **Servings:** 4

Ingredients:

- 2 egg yolks
- Salt and black pepper to the taste
- ¼ cup ghee
- 1 tbsp. lemon juice
- A pinch of cayenne pepper
- 40 asparagus spears

Instructions:

1. In a bowl, whisk egg yolks very well.

2. Transfer this to a small pan over low heat.

3. Add lemon juice and whisk well.

4. Add ghee and whisk until it melts.

5. Add salt, pepper and cayenne pepper and whisk again well.

6. Meanwhile, heat up a pan over medium high heat, add asparagus spears and fry them for 5 minutes.

7. Divide asparagus on plates, drizzle the sauce you've made on

top and serve.

Nutrition: cal. 150, fat 13, fiber 6, carbs 2, protein 3

8. <u>Shrimp Pasta</u>

Preparation time: 10 minutes **Cooking time:** 10 minutes **Servings:** 4

Ingredients:

- 12 ounces angel hair noodles
- 2 tbsp. olive oil
- Salt and black pepper to the taste
- 2 tbsp. ghee
- 4 garlic cloves, minced
- 1 pound shrimp, raw, peeled and deveined
- Juice of ½ lemon
- ½ tsp. paprika
- A handful basil, chopped

Instructions:

1. Put water in a pot, add some salt, bring to a boil, add noodles, cook for 2 minutes, drain them and transfer to a heated pan.

2. Toast noodles for a few seconds, take off heat and leave them aside.

3. Heat up a pan with the ghee and olive oil over medium heat, add garlic, stir and brown for 1 minute.

4. Add shrimp and lemon juice and cook for 3 minutes on each side.

5. Add noodles, salt, pepper and paprika, stir, divide into bowls and serve with chopped basil on top.

Nutrition: cal. 300, fat 20, fiber 6, carbs 3, protein 30

9. <u>Mexican Casserole</u>

Preparation time: 10 minutes **Cooking time:** 35 minutes **Servings:** 6

Ingredients:

- 2 chipotle peppers, chopped
- 2 jalapenos, chopped
- 1 tbsp. olive oil
- ¼ cup heavy cream
- 1 small white onion, chopped
- Salt and black pepper to the taste

- 1 pound chicken thighs, skinless, boneless and chopped
- 1 cup red enchilada sauce
- 4 ounces cream cheese
- Cooking spray
- 1 cup pepper jack cheese, shredded
- 2 tbsp. cilantro, chopped
- 2 tortillas

Instructions:

1. Heat up a pan with the oil over medium heat, add chipotle and jalapeno peppers, stir and cook for a few seconds.

2. Add onion, stir and cook for 5 minutes.

3. Add cream cheese and heavy cream and stir until cheese melts.

4. Add chicken, salt, pepper and enchilada sauce, stir well and

take off heat.

5. Grease a baking dish with cooking spray, place tortillas on the bottom, spread chicken mix all over and sprinkle shredded cheese.

6. Cover with tin foil, introduce in the oven at 350 degrees F and bake for 15 minutes.

7. Remove the tin foil and bake for 15 minutes more.

8. Sprinkle cilantro on top and serve.

Nutrition: cal.240, fat 12, fiber 5, carbs 5, protein 20

Side Dishes & Dinner Recipes

10. <u>**Brussels Sprouts Side Dish**</u>

Preparation time: 10 minutes **Cooking time:** 10 minutes **Servings:** 4

Ingredients:

- 1 pound Brussels sprouts, trimmed and halved
- Salt and black pepper to the taste

- 1 tsp. sesame seeds
- 1 tbsp. green onions, chopped
- 1 and ½ tbsp. sukrin gold syrup
- 1 tbsp. coconut aminos
- 2 tbsp. sesame oil
- 1 tbsp. sriracha

Instructions:

1. In a bowl, mix sesame oil with coconut aminos, sriracha, syrup, salt and black pepper and whisk well.

2. Heat up a pan over medium high heat, add Brussels sprouts and cook them for 5 minutes on each side.

3. Add sesame oil mix, toss to coat, sprinkle sesame seeds and green onions, stir again and serve as a side dish.

Nutrition: cal.110, fat 4, fiber 4, carbs 6, protein 4

11. <u>Pesto</u>

Preparation time: 10 minutes **Cooking time:** 0 minutes **Servings:** 4

Ingredients:

- ½ cup olive oil
- 2 cups basil
- 1/3 cup pine nuts
- 1/3 cup parmesan cheese, grated
- 2 garlic cloves, chopped
- Salt and black pepper to the taste

Instructions:

1. Put basil in your food processor, add pine nuts and garlic and

blend very well.

2. Add parmesan, salt, pepper and the oil gradually and blend again until you

obtain a paste.

3. Serve with chicken!

Nutrition: cal.100, fat 7, fiber 3, carbs 1, protein 5

12. <u>Brussels Sprouts And Bacon</u>

Preparation time: 10 minutes **Cooking time:** 30 minutes **Servings:** 4

Ingredients:

- 8 bacon strips, chopped
- 1 pound Brussels sprouts, trimmed and halved
- Salt and black pepper to the taste
- A pinch of cumin, ground

- A pinch of red pepper, crushed
- 2 tbsp. extra virgin olive oil

Instructions:

1. In a bowl, mix Brussels sprouts with salt, pepper, cumin, red

pepper and oil and toss to coat.

2. Spread Brussels sprouts on a lined baking sheet, introduce in

the oven at 375 degrees F and bake for 30 minutes.

3. Meanwhile, heat up a pan over medium heat, add bacon pieces

and cook them until they become crispy.

4. Divide baked Brussels sprouts on plates, top with bacon and

serve as a side dish right away.

Nutrition: cal.256, fat 20, fiber 6, carbs 5, protein 15

13. <u>Spinach Side Dish</u>

Preparation time: 10 minutes **Cooking time:** 15 minutes **Servings:** 2

Ingredients:

- 2 garlic cloves, minced
- 8 ounces spinach leaves
- A drizzle of olive oil
- Salt and black pepper to the taste
- 4 tbsp. sour cream
- 1 tbsp. ghee
- 2 tbsp. parmesan cheese, grated

Instructions:

1. Heat up a pan with the oil over medium heat, add spinach, stir and cook until it softens.

2. Add salt, pepper, ghee, parmesan and ghee, stir and cook for 4 minutes.

3. Add sour cream, stir and cook for 5 minutes more.

4. Divide between plates and serve as a side dish.

Nutrition: cal. 133, fat 10, fiber 4, carbs 4, protein 2

14. **Avocado Fries**

Preparation time: 10 minutes **Cooking time:** 5 minutes **Servings:** 3

Ingredients:

- 3 avocados, pitted, peeled, halved and sliced
- 1 and ½ cups sunflower oil
- 1 and ½ cups almond meal
- A pinch of cayenne pepper
- Salt and black pepper to the taste

Instructions:

1. In a bowl mix almond meal with salt, pepper and cayenne and

stir.

2. In a second bowl, whisk eggs with a pinch of salt and pepper.

3. Dredge avocado pieces in egg and then in almond meal mix.

4. Heat up a pan with the oil over medium high heat, add avocado fries and cook them until they are golden.

5. Transfer to paper towels, drain grease and divide between plates.

6. Serve as a side dish.

Nutrition: cal.450, fat 43, fiber 4, carbs 7, protein 17

15. __Roasted Cauliflower__

Preparation time: 10 minutes **Cooking time:** 25 minutes **Servings:** 6

Ingredients:

- 1 cauliflower head, florets separated
- Salt and black pepper to the taste
- 1/3 cup parmesan, grated
- 1 tbsp. parsley, chopped
- 3 tbsp. olive oil
- 2 tbsp. extra virgin olive oil

Instructions:

1. In a bowl, mix oil with garlic, salt, pepper and cauliflower florets.

2. Toss to coat well, spread this on a lined baking sheet, introduce in the oven at 450 degrees F and bake for 25 minutes, stirring halfway.

3. Add parmesan and parsley, stir and cook for 5 minutes more.

4. Divide between plates and serve as a keto side dish.

Nutrition: cal.118, fat 2, fiber 3, carbs 1, protein 6

16. __Mushroom And Spinach Side Dish__

Preparation time: 10 minutes **Cooking time:** 10 minutes **Servings:** 4

Ingredients:

- 10 ounces spinach leaves, chopped
- Salt and black pepper to the taste
- 14 ounces mushrooms, chopped
- 2 garlic cloves, minced
- A handful parsley, chopped
- 1 yellow onion, chopped
- 4 tbsp. olive oil
- 2 tbsp. balsamic vinegar

Instructions:

1. Heat up a pan with the oil over medium high heat, add garlic and onion, stir and cook for 4 minutes.

2. Add mushrooms, stir and cook for 3 minutes more.

3. Add spinach, stir and cook for 3 minutes.

4. Add vinegar, salt and pepper, stir and cook for 1 minute more.

5. Add parsley, stir, divide between plates and serve hot as a side dish.

Nutrition: cal. 200, fat 4, fiber 6, carbs 2, protein 12

17. **Okra And Tomatoes**

Preparation time: 10 minutes **Cooking time:** 10 minutes **Servings:** 6

Ingredients:

- 14 ounces canned stewed tomatoes, chopped
- Salt and black pepper to the taste
- 2 celery stalks, chopped
- 1 yellow onion, chopped
- 1 pound okra, sliced
- 2 bacon slices, chopped
- 1 small green bell peppers, chopped

Instructions:

1. Heat up a pan over medium high heat, add bacon, stir, brown for a few minutes, transfer to paper towels and leave aside for now.

2. Heat up the pan again over medium heat, add okra, bell pepper, onion and celery, stir and cook for 2 minutes.

3. Add tomatoes, salt and pepper, stir and cook for 3 minutes.

4. Divide on plates, garnish with crispy bacon and serve.

Nutrition: cal.100, fat 2, fiber 3, carbs 2, protein 6

18.   **Snap Peas And Mint**

Preparation time: 10 minutes **Cooking time:** 5 minutes **Servings:** 4

Ingredients:

- ¾ pound sugar snap peas, trimmed
- Salt and black pepper to the taste
- 1 tbsp. mint leaves, chopped
- 2 tsp. olive oil
- 3 green onions, chopped
- 1 garlic clove, minced

Instructions:

1. Heat up a pan with the oil over medium high heat.

2. Add snap peas, salt, pepper, green onions, garlic and mint.

3. Stir everything, cook for 5 minutes, divide between plates and serve as a side dish for a pork steak.

Nutrition: cal.70, fat 1, fiber 1, carbs 0.4, protein 6

19. Collard Greens Side Dish

Preparation time: 10 minutes **Cooking time:** 2 hours and 15 minutes

Servings: 10

Ingredients:

- 5 bunches collard greens, chopped
- Salt and black pepper to the taste
- 1 tbsp. red pepper flakes, crushed
- 5 cups chicken stock
- 1 turkey leg
- 2 tbsp. garlic, minced
- ¼ cup olive oil

Instructions:

1. Heat up a pot with the oil over medium heat, add garlic, stir and cook for 1 minute.

2. Add stock, salt, pepper and turkey leg, stir, cover and simmer for 30 minutes.

3. Add collard greens, cover pot again and cook for 45 minutes more.

4. Reduce heat to medium, add more salt and pepper, stir and cook for 1 hour.

5. Drain greens, mix them with red pepper flakes, stir, divide between plates and serve as a side dish.

Nutrition: cal.143, fat 3, fiber 4, carbs 3, protein 6

Seafoods Recipes

20. **Octopus Salad**

Preparation time: 10 minutes **Cooking time:** 40 minutes **Servings:** 2

Ingredients:

- 21 ounces octopus, rinsed
- Juice of 1 lemon
- 4 celery stalks, chopped
- 3 ounces olive oil
- Salt and black pepper to the taste
- 4 tbsp. parsley, chopped

Instructions:

1. Put the octopus in a pot, add water to cover, cover pot, bring to a boil over medium heat, cook for 40 minutes, drain and leave aside to cool down.

2. Chop octopus and put it in a salad bowl.

3. Add celery stalks, parsley, oil and lemon juice and toss well.

4. Season with salt and pepper, toss again and serve.

Nutrition: cal. 140, fat 10, fiber 3, carbs 6, protein 23

21.   <u>**Clam Chowder**</u>

Preparation time: 10 minutes **Cooking time:** 2 hours **Servings:** 4

Ingredients:

- 1 cup celery stalks, chopped
- Salt and black pepper to the taste
- 1 tsp. thyme, ground
- 2 cups chicken stock
- 14 ounces canned baby clams
- 2 cups whipping cream
- 1 cup onion, chopped
- 13 bacon slices, chopped

Instructions:

1. Heat up a pan over medium heat, add bacon slices, brown them and transfer to a bowl.

2. Heat up the same pan over medium heat, add celery and onion, stir and cook for 5 minutes.

3. Transfer everything to your Crockpot, also add bacon, baby clams, salt, pepper, stock, thyme and whipping cream, stir and cook on High for 2 hours.

4. Divide into bowls and serve.

Nutrition: cal.420, fat 22, fiber 0, carbs 5, protein 25

22.   Flounder And Shrimp

Preparation time: 10 minutes **Cooking time:** 20 minutes **Servings:** 4

Ingredients: *For the seasoning:*

- 2 tsp. onion powder
- 2 tsp. thyme, dried
- 2 tsp. sweet paprika
- 2 tsp. garlic powder
- Salt and black pepper to the taste
- ½ tsp. allspice, ground
- 1 tsp. oregano, dried
- A pinch of cayenne pepper
- ¼ tsp. nutmeg, ground
- ¼ tsp. cloves
- A pinch of cinnamon powder
- *For the etouffee:*
- 2 shallots, chopped
- 1 tbsp. ghee
- 8 ounces bacon, sliced
- 1 green bell pepper, chopped
- 1 celery stick, chopped
- 2 tbsp. coconut flour
- 1 tomato, chopped
- 4 garlic cloves, minced
- 8 ounces shrimp, peeled, deveined and chopped

- 2 cups chicken stock
- 1 tbsp. coconut milk
- A handful parsley, chopped
- 1 tsp. Tabasco sauce
- Salt and black pepper to the taste
- *For the flounder:*
- 4 flounder fillets
- 2 tbsp. ghee

Instructions:

1. In a bowl, mix paprika with thyme, garlic and onion powder, salt, pepper, oregano, allspice, cayenne pepper, cloves, nutmeg and cinnamon and stir.

2. Reserve 2 tbsp. of this mix, rub the flounder with the rest and leave aside.

3. Heat up a pan over medium heat, add bacon, stir and cook for 6 minutes.

4. Add celery, bell pepper, shallots and 1 tbsp. ghee, stir and cook for 4 minutes.

5. Add tomato and garlic, stir and cook for 4 minutes.

6. Add coconut flour and reserved seasoning, stir and cook for 2 minutes more.

7. Add chicken stock and bring to a simmer.

8. Meanwhile, heat up a pan with 2 tbsp. ghee over medium high heat, add fish, cook for 2 minutes, flip and cut for 2 minutes more.

9. Add shrimp to the pan with the stock, stir and cook for 2 minutes.

10. Add parsley, salt, pepper, coconut milk and Tabasco sauce, stir and take off heat.

11. Divide fish on plates, top with the shrimp sauce and serve.

Nutrition: cal. 200, fat 5, fiber 7, carbs 4, protein 20

23. **Shrimp Salad**

Preparation time: 10 minutes **Cooking time:** 10 minutes **Servings:** 4

Ingredients:

- 2 tbsp. olive oil
- 1 pound shrimp, peeled and deveined
- Salt and black pepper to the taste
- 2 tbsp. lime juice
- 3 endives, leaves separated
- 3 tbsp. parsley, chopped
- 2 tsp. mint, chopped
- 1 tbsp. tarragon, chopped

- 1 tbsp. lemon juice
- 2 tbsp. mayonnaise
- 1 tsp. lime zest
- ½ cup sour cream

Instructions:

1. In a bowl, mix shrimp with salt, pepper and the olive oil, toss to coat and spread them on a lined baking sheet.

2. Introduce shrimp in the oven at 400 degrees F and bake for 10 minutes.

3. Add lime juice, toss them to coat again and leave aside for now.

4. In a bowl, mix mayo with sour cream, lime zest, lemon juice, salt, pepper, tarragon, mint and parsley and stir very well.

5. Chop shrimp, add to salad dressing, toss to coat everything and spoon into endive leaves.

6. Serve right away.

Nutrition: cal.200, fat 11, fiber 2, carbs 1, protein 13

24. Delicious Oysters

Preparation time: 10 minutes **Cooking time:** 0 minutes **Servings:** 4

Ingredients:

- 12 oysters, shucked
- Juice of 1 lemon
- Juice from 1 orange
- Zest from 1 orange
- Juice from 1 lime
- Zest from 1 lime
- 2 tbsp. ketchup
- 1 Serrano chili pepper, chopped
- 1 cup tomato juice
- ½ tsp. ginger, grated
- ¼ tsp. garlic, minced
- Salt to the taste
- ¼ cup olive oil
- ¼ cup cilantro, chopped
- ¼ cup scallions, chopped

Instructions:

1. In a bowl, mix lemon juice, orange juice, orange zest, lime juice and zest, ketchup, chili pepper, tomato juice, ginger, garlic, oil, scallions, cilantro and salt and stir well. Spoon this into oysters and serve them.

Nutrition: cal.100, fat 1, fiber 0, carbs 2, protein 5

25. <u>Salmon Rolls</u>

Preparation time: 10 minutes **Cooking time:** 0 minutes **Servings:** 12

Ingredients:

- 2 nori seeds
- 1 small avocado, pitted, peeled and finely chopped
- 6 ounces smoked salmon. Sliced
- 4 ounces cream cheese

- 1 cucumber, sliced
- 1 tsp. wasabi paste
- Picked ginger for serving

Instructions:

1. Place nori sheets on a sushi mat.

2. Divide salmon slices on them and also avocado and cucumber slices.

3. In a bowl, mix cream cheese with wasabi paste and stir well.

4. Spread this over cucumber slices, roll your nori sheets, press well, cut each into 6 pieces and serve with pickled ginger.

Nutrition: cal.80, fat 6, fiber 1, carbs 2, protein 4

26. **Salmon Skewers**

Preparation time: 10 minutes **Cooking time:** 8 minutes **Servings:** 4

Ingredients:

- 12 ounces salmon fillet, cubed
- 1 red onion, cut into chunks
- ½ red bell pepper cut in chunks
- ½ green bell pepper cut in chunks
- ½ orange bell pepper cut in chunks
- Juice from 1 lemon
- Salt and black pepper to the taste
- A drizzle of olive oil

Instructions:

1. Thread skewers with onion, red, green and orange pepper and

salmon cubes.

2. Season them with salt and pepper, drizzle oil and lemon juice and place them on preheated grill over medium high heat.

3. Cook for 4 minutes on each side, divide between plates and serve.

Nutrition: cal. 150, fat 3, fiber 6, carbs 3, protein 8

Poultry Recipes

27. **Chicken Casserole**

Preparation time: 10 minutes **Cooking time:** 45 minutes **Servings:** 4

Ingredients:

- 3 cups cheddar cheese, grated
- 10 ounces broccoli florets
- 3 chicken breasts, skinless, boneless, cooked and cubed
- 1 cup mayo
- 1 tbsp. coconut oil, melted
- 1/3 cup chicken stock

- Salt and black pepper to the taste
- Juice of 1 lemon

Instructions:

1. Grease a baking dish with oil and arrange chicken pieces on the bottom.

2. Spread broccoli florets and then half of the cheese.

3. In a bowl, mix mayo with stock, salt, pepper and lemon juice.

4. Pour this over chicken, sprinkle the rest of the cheese, cover dish with tin foil and bake in the oven at 350 degrees F for 30 minutes

5. Remove foil and bake for 20 minutes more.

6. Serve hot.

Nutrition: cal.250, fat 5, fiber 4, carbs 6, protein 25

28. <u>Creamy Chicken Soup</u>

Preparation time: 10 minutes **Cooking time:** 20 minutes **Servings:** 4

Ingredients:

- 3 tbsp. ghee
- 4 ounces cream cheese
- 2 cups chicken meat, cooked and shredded
- 1/3 cup red sauce

- 4 cups chicken stock
- Salt and black pepper to the taste
- ½ cup sour cream
- ¼ cup celery, chopped

Instructions:

1. In your blender, mix stock with red sauce, cream cheese, ghee,

salt, pepper and sour cream and pulse well.

2. Transfer this to a pot, heat up over medium heat and add celery

and chicken.

3. Stir, simmer for a few minutes, divide into bowls and serve.

Nutrition: cal.400, fat 23, fiber 5, carbs 5, protein 30

29. **Chicken Crepes**

Preparation time: 10 minutes **Cooking time:** 30 minutes **Servings:** 8

Ingredients:

6 eggs

6 ounces cream cheese

1 tsp. erythritol

- 1 and ½ tbsp. coconut flour
- 1/3 cup parmesan, grated
- A pinch of xanthan gum
- Cooking spray

- *For the filling:*
- 8 ounces spinach
- 8 ounces mushrooms, sliced
- 8 ounces rotisserie chicken, shredded
- 8 ounces cheese blend
- 2 ounces cream cheese
- 1 garlic clove, minced
- 1 small yellow onion, chopped
- *Liquids:*
- 2 tbsp. red wine vinegar
- 2 tbsp. ghee
- ½ cup heavy cream
- 1 tsp. Worcestershire sauce
- ¼ cup chicken stock
- A pinch of nutmeg
- Chopped parsley
- Salt and black pepper to the taste

Instructions: 1. In a bowl, mix 6 ounces cream cheese with eggs, parm,

erythritol, xanthan and coconut flour and stir very well until

you obtain a crepes batter.

2. Heat up a pan over medium heat, spray some cooking oil, pour

some of the batters, spread well into the pan, cook for 2

minutes, flip and cook for 30 seconds more.

3. Repeat with the rest of the batter and place all crepes on a

plate.

4. Heat up a pan with 2 tbsp. ghee over medium high heat,

add onion, stir and cook for 2 minutes.

5. Add garlic, stir and cook for 1 minute more.

6. Add mushrooms, stir and cook for 2 minutes.

7. Add chicken, spinach, salt, pepper, stock, vinegar, nutmeg,

Worcestershire sauce, heavy cream, 2 ounces cream cheese

and 6-ounce cheese blend, stir everything and cook for 7

minutes more.

8. Fill each crepe with this mix, roll them and arrange them all in

a baking dish.

9. Top with 2 ounces cheese blend, introduce in preheated broiler

for a couple of minutes.

10. Divide crepes on plates, top with chopped parsley and serve.

Nutrition: cal. 360, fat 32, fiber 2, carbs 7, protein 20

30. **Awesome Chicken Dish**

Preparation time: 10 minutes **Cooking time:** 50 minutes **Servings:** 4

Ingredients:

- 3 pounds chicken breasts
- 2 ounces muenster cheese, cubed
- 2 ounces cream cheese
- 4 ounces cheddar cheese, cubed
- 2 ounces provolone cheese, cubed
- 1 zucchini, shredded
- Salt and black pepper to the taste
- 1 tsp. garlic, minced
- ½ cup bacon, cooked and crumbled

Instructions:

1. Season zucchini with salt and pepper, leave aside few minutes,

squeeze well and transfer to a bowl.

2. Add bacon, garlic, more salt and pepper, cream cheese,

cheddar cheese, muenster cheese and provolone cheese and

stir.

3. Cut slits into chicken breasts, season with salt and pepper and

stuff with zucchini and cheese mix.

4. Place on a lined baking sheet, introduce in the oven at 400 degrees F and bake for 45 minutes.

5. Divide between plates and serve.

Nutrition: cal.455, fat 20, fiber 0, carbs 2, protein 57

31. <u>Crusted Chicken</u>

Preparation time: 10 minutes **Cooking time:** 35 minutes **Servings:** 4

Ingredients:

- 4 bacon slices, cooked and crumbled
- 4 chicken breasts, skinless and boneless
- 1 tbsp. water
- ½ cup avocado oil
- 1 egg, whisked
- Salt and black pepper to the taste
- 1 cup asiago cheese, shredded
- ¼ tsp. garlic powder
- 1 cup parmesan cheese, grated

Instructions:

1. In a bowl, mix parmesan cheese with garlic, salt and pepper and stir.

2. Put whisked egg in another bowl and mix with the water.

3. Season chicken with salt and pepper and dip each piece into egg and then into cheese mix.

4. Heat up a pan with the oil over medium high heat, add chicken breasts, cook until they are golden on both sides and transfer to a baking pan.

5. Introduce in the oven at 350 degrees F and bake for 20 minutes.

6. Top chicken with bacon and asiago cheese, introduce in the oven, turn on broiler and broil for a couple of minutes.

7. Serve hot.

Nutrition: cal.400, fat 22, fiber 1, carbs 1, protein 47

32.   **Cheesy Chicken**

Preparation time: 10 minutes **Cooking time:** 30 minutes **Servings:** 4

Ingredients:

- 1 zucchini, chopped
- Salt and black pepper to the taste
- 1 tsp. garlic powder
- 1 tbsp. avocado oil
- 2 chicken breasts, skinless and boneless and sliced
- 1 tomato, chopped
- ½ tsp. oregano, dried
- ½ tsp. basil, dried
- ½ cup mozzarella cheese, shredded

Instructions:

1. Season chicken with salt, pepper and garlic powder.

2. Heat up a pan with the oil over medium heat, add chicken

slices, brown on all sides and transfer them to a baking dish.

3. Heat up the pan again over medium heat, add zucchini,

oregano, tomato, basil, salt and pepper, stir, cook for 2 minutes

and pour over chicken.

4. Introduce in the oven at 325 degrees F and bake for 20

minutes.

5. Spread mozzarella over chicken, introduce in the oven again

and bake for 5 minutes more.

6. Divide between plates and serve.

Nutrition: cal. 235, fat 4, fiber 1, carbs 2, protein 35

33. <u>Orange Chicken</u>

Preparation time: 10 minutes **Cooking time:** 15 minutes **Servings:** 4

Ingredients:

- 2 pounds chicken thighs, skinless, boneless and cut into pieces
- Salt and black pepper to the taste
- 3 tbsp. coconut oil
- ¼ cup coconut flour
- *For the sauce:*
- 2 tbsp. fish sauce
- 1 and ½ tsp. orange extract
- 1 tbsp. ginger, grated
- ¼ cup orange juice

- 2 tsp. stevia
- 1 tbsp. orange zest
- ¼ tsp. sesame seeds
- 2 tbsp. scallions, chopped
- ½ tsp. coriander, ground
- 1 cup water
- ¼ tsp. red pepper flakes
- 2 tbsp. gluten free soy sauce

Instructions:

1. In a bowl, mix coconut flour and salt and pepper and stir.

2. Add chicken pieces and toss to coat well.

3. Heat up a pan with the oil over medium heat, add chicken, cook until they are golden on both sides and transfer to a bowl.

4. In your blender, mix orange juice with ginger, fish sauce, soy sauce, stevia, orange extract, water and coriander and blend well.

5. Pour this into a pan and heat up over medium heat.

6. Add chicken, stir and cook for 2 minutes.

7. Add sesame seeds, orange zest, scallions and pepper flakes, stir

cook for 2 minutes and take off heat.

8. Divide between plates and serve.

Nutrition: cal.423, fat 20, fiber 5, carbs 6, protein 45

Meat Recipes

34. <u>Ground Beef Casserole</u>

Preparation time: 10 minutes **Cooking time:** 35 minutes **Servings:** 6

Ingredients:

- 2 tsp. onion flakes
- 1 tbsp. gluten free Worcestershire sauce
- 2 pounds beef, ground
- 2 garlic cloves, minced
- Salt and black pepper to the taste
- 1 cup mozzarella cheese, shredded
- 2 cups cheddar cheese, shredded

- 1 cup Russian dressing
- 2 tbsp. sesame seeds, toasted
- 20 dill pickle slices
- 1 romaine lettuce head, torn

Instructions:

1. Heat up a pan over medium heat, add beef, onion flakes,

Worcestershire sauce, salt, pepper and garlic, stir and cook for

5 minutes.

2. Transfer this to a baking dish, add 1 cup cheddar cheese over it

and also the mozzarella and half of the Russian dressing.

3. Stir and spread evenly.

4. Arrange pickle slices on top, sprinkle the rest of the cheddar

and the sesame seeds, introduce in the oven at 350 degrees f

and bake for 20 minutes.

5. Turn oven to broil and broil the casserole for 5 minutes more.

6. Divide lettuce on plates, top with a beef casserole and the rest

of the Russian dressing.

Nutrition: cal.554, fat 51, fiber 3, carbs 5, protein 45

35. Zoodles And Beef

Preparation time: 10 minutes **Cooking time:** 20 minutes **Servings:** 5

Ingredients:

- 1 pound beef, ground
- 1 yellow onion, chopped
- 2 garlic cloves, minced
- 14 ounces canned tomatoes, chopped
- 1 tbsp. rosemary, dried
- 1 tbsp. sage, dried
- 1 tbsp. oregano, dried
- 1 tbsp. basil, dried
- 1 tbsp. marjoram, dried
- Salt and black pepper to the taste
- 2 zucchinis, cut with a spiralizer

Instructions:

1. Heat up a pan over medium heat, add garlic and onion, stir and brown for a couple of minutes.

2. Add beef, stir and cook for 6 minutes more.

3. Add tomatoes, salt, pepper, rosemary, sage, oregano, marjoram and basil, stir and simmer for 15 minutes. Divide zoodles into bowls, add beef mix and serve.

Nutrition: cal. 320, fat 13, fiber 4, carbs 12, protein 40

36. **Jamaican Beef Pies**

Preparation time: 10 minutes **Cooking time:** 35 minutes **Servings:** 12

Ingredients:

- 3 garlic cloves, minced
- ½ pound beef, ground
- ½ pound pork, ground
- ½ cup water
- 1 small onion, chopped
- 2 habanero peppers, chopped
- 1 tsp. Jamaican curry powder
- 1 tsp. thyme, dried
- 2 tsp. coriander, ground

- ½ tsp. allspice
- 2 tsp. cumin, ground
- ½ tsp. turmeric
- A pinch of cloves, ground
- Salt and black pepper to the taste
- 1 tsp. garlic powder
- ¼ tsp. stevia powder
- 2 tbsp. ghee
- *For the crust:*
- 4 tbsp. ghee, melted
- 6 ounces cream cheese
- A pinch of salt
- 1 tsp. turmeric
- ¼ tsp. stevia
- ½ tsp. baking powder
- 1 and ½ cups flax meal
- 2 tbsp. water
- ½ cup coconut flour

Instructions:

1. In your blender, mix onion with habaneros, garlic and ½ cup

water.

2. Heat up a pan over medium heat, add pork and beef meat, stir and cook for 3 minutes.

3. Add onions mix, stir and cook for 2 minutes more.

4. Add garlic, onion, curry powder, ½ tsp. turmeric, thyme, coriander, cumin, allspice, cloves, salt, pepper, stevia powder and garlic powder, stir well and cook for 3 minutes.

5. Add 2 tbsp. ghee, stir until it melts and take this off heat.

6. Meanwhile, in a bowl, mix 1 tsp. turmeric, with ¼ tsp. stevia, baking powder, flax meal and coconut flour and stir.

7. In a separate bowl, mix 4 tbsp. ghee with 2 tbsp. water and cream cheese and stir.

8. Combine the 2 mixtures and mix until you obtain a dough.

9. Shape 12 balls from this mix, place them on a parchment paper and roll each into a circle.

10. Divide beef and pork mix on one half of the dough circles, cover with the other halves, seal edges and arrange them all on a lined baking sheet.

11. Bake your pies in the oven at 350 degrees F for 25 minutes.

12. Serve them warm.

Nutrition: cal.267, fat 23, fiber 1, carbs 3, protein 12

37. Amazing Goulash

Preparation time: 10 minutes **Cooking time:** 20 minutes **Servings:** 5

Ingredients:

- 2 ounces bell pepper, chopped
- 1 and ½ pounds beef, ground
- Salt and black pepper to the taste
- 2 cups cauliflower florets
- ¼ cup onion, chopped
- 14 ounces canned tomatoes and their juice
- ¼ tsp. garlic powder
- 1 tbsp. tomato paste
- 14 ounces water

Instructions:

1. Heat up a pan over medium heat, add beef, stir and brown for 5 minutes.

2. Add onion and bell pepper, stir and cook for 4 minutes more.

3. Add cauliflower, tomatoes and their juice and water, stir, bring to a simmer, cover pan and cook for 5 minutes.

4. Add tomato paste, garlic powder, salt and pepper, stir, take off heat, divide into bowls and serve.

Nutrition: cal.275, fat 7, fiber 2, carbs 4, protein 10

38. Beef And Eggplant Casserole

Preparation time: 30 minutes **Cooking time:** 4 hours **Servings:** 12

Ingredients:

1 tbsp. olive oil

2 pounds beef, ground

2 cups eggplant, chopped

Salt and black pepper to the taste

2 tsp. mustard

2 tsp. gluten free Worcestershire sauce

28 ounces canned tomatoes, chopped

2 cups mozzarella, grated

16 ounces tomato sauce

2 tbsp. parsley, chopped

1 tsp. oregano, dried

Instructions:

1. Season eggplant pieces with salt and pepper, leave them aside for 30 minutes, squeeze water a bit, put them into a bowl, add the olive oil and toss them to coat.

2. In another bowl, mix beef with salt, pepper, mustard and Worcestershire sauce and stir well.

3. Press them on the bottom of a crock pot.

4. Add eggplant and spread.

5. Also add tomatoes, tomato sauce, parsley, oregano and mozzarella.

6. Cover Crockpot and cook on Low for 4 hours.

7. Divide casserole between plates and serve hot.

Nutrition: cal. 200, fat 12, fiber 2, carbs 6, protein 15

39. **Braised Lamb Chops**

Preparation time: 10 minutes **Cooking time:** 2 hours and 20 minutes
Servings:4

Ingredients:

- 8 lamb chops
- 1 tsp. garlic powder
- Salt and black pepper to the taste
- 2 tsp. mint, crushed
- A drizzle of olive oil
- 1 shallot, chopped
- 1 cup white wine
- Juice of ½ lemon
- 1 bay leaf
- 2 cups beef stock
- Some chopped parsley for serving
- *For the sauce:*
- 2 cups cranberries
- ½ tsp. rosemary, chopped
- ½ cup swerve
- 1 tsp. mint, dried
- Juice of ½ lemon
- 1 tsp. ginger, grated
- 1 cup water
- 1 tsp. harissa paste

Instructions:

1. In a bowl, mix lamb chops with salt, pepper, 1 tsp. garlic powder and 2 tsp. mint and rub well.

2. Heat up a pan with a drizzle of oil over medium high heat, add lamb chops, brown them on all sides and transfer to a plate.

3. Heat up the same pan again over medium high heat, add shallots, stir and cook for 1 minute.

4. Add wine and bay leaf, stir and cook for 4 minutes.

5. Add 2 cups beef stock, parsley and juice from ½ lemon, stir and simmer for 5 minutes.

6. Return lamb, stir and cook for 10 minutes.

7. Cover pan and introduce it in the oven at 350 degrees F for 2 hours.

8. Meanwhile, heat up a pan over medium high heat, add cranberries, swerve, rosemary, 1 tsp. mint, juice from ½ lemon, ginger, water and harissa paste, stir, bring to a simmer for 15 minutes.

9. Take lamb chops out of the oven, divide them between plates, drizzle the cranberry sauce over them and serve.

Nutrition: cal.450, fat 34, fiber 2, carbs 6, protein 26

40. <u>Lamb Salad</u>

Preparation time: 10 minutes **Cooking time:** 35 minutes **Servings:** 4

Ingredients:

- 1 tbsp. olive oil
- 3 pounds leg of lamb, bone discarded and butterflied
- Salt and black pepper to the taste
- 1 tsp. cumin, ground
- A pinch of thyme, dried
- 2 garlic cloves, minced
- *For the salad:*
- 4 ounces feta cheese, crumbled
- ½ cup pecans

84

- 2 cups spinach
- 1 and ½ tbsp. lemon juice
- ¼ cup olive oil
- 1 cup mint, chopped

Instructions:

1. Rub lamb with salt, pepper, 1 tbsp. oil, thyme, cumin and minced garlic, place on preheated grill over medium high heat and cook for 40 minutes, flipping once.

2. Meanwhile, spread pecans on a lined baking sheet, introduce in the oven at 350 degrees F and toast for 10 minutes.

3. Transfer grilled lamb to a cutting board, leave aside to cool down and slice.

4. In a salad bowl, mix spinach with 1 cup mint, feta cheese, ¼ cup olive oil, lemon juice, toasted pecans, salt and pepper and toss to coat.

5. Add lamb slices on top and serve.

Nutrition: cal.334, fat 33, fiber 3, carbs 5, protein 7

Vegetable Recipes

41. **Crispy Radishes**

Preparation time: 10 minutes **Cooking time:** 20 minutes **Servings:** 4

Ingredients:

- Cooking spray
- 15 radishes, sliced
- Salt and black pepper to the taste
- 1 tbsp. chives, chopped

Instructions:

1. Arrange radish slices on a lined baking sheet and spray them

with cooking oil.

2. Season with salt and pepper and sprinkle chives, introduce in

the oven at 375 degrees F and bake for 10 minutes.

3. Flip them and bake for 10 minutes more.

4. Serve them cold.

Nutrition: cal.30, fat 1, fiber 0.4, carbs 1, protein 0.1

42. <u>Creamy Radishes</u>

Preparation time: 10 minutes **Cooking time:** 25 minutes **Servings:** 1

Ingredients:

- 7 ounces radishes, cut in halves
- 2 tbsp. sour cream
- 2 bacon slices
- 1 tbsp. green onion, chopped

- 1 tbsp. cheddar cheese, grated
- Hot sauce to the taste
- Salt and black pepper to the taste

Instructions:

1. Put radishes into a pot, add water to cover, bring to a boil over medium heat, cook them for 10 minutes and drain.

2. Heat up a pan over medium high heat, add bacon, cook until it's crispy, transfer to paper towels, drain grease, crumble and leave aside.

3. Return pan to medium heat, add radishes, stir and sauté them

for 7 minutes.

4. Add onion, salt, pepper, hot sauce and sour cream, stir and cook for 7 minutes more.

5. Transfer to a plate, top with crumbled bacon and cheddar cheese and serve.

Nutrition: cal. 340, fat 23, fiber 3, carbs 6, protein 15

43. **Radish Soup**

Preparation time: 10 minutes **Cooking time:** 20 minutes **Servings:** 4

Ingredients:

- 2 bunches radishes, cut in quarters
- Salt and black pepper to the taste
- 6 cups chicken stock
- 2 stalks celery, chopped
- 3 tbsp. coconut oil
- 6 garlic cloves, minced
- 1 yellow onion, chopped

Instructions:

1. Heat up a pot with the oil over medium heat, add onion, celery and garlic, stir and cook for 5 minutes.

2. Add radishes, stock, salt and pepper, stir, bring to a boil, cover and simmer for 15 minutes.

3. Divide into soup bowls and serve.

Nutrition: cal.120, fat 2, fiber 1, carbs 3, protein 10

44. <u>Avocado Salad</u>

Preparation time: 10 minutes **Cooking time:** 0 minutes **Servings:** 4

Ingredients:

- 2 avocados, pitted and mashed
- Salt and black pepper to the taste
- ¼ tsp. lemon stevia
- 1 tbsp. white vinegar
- 14 ounces coleslaw mix
- Juice from 2 limes
- ¼ cup red onion, chopped
- ¼ cup cilantro, chopped

- 2 tbsp. olive oil

Instructions:

1. Put coleslaw mix in a salad bowl.

Add avocado mash and onions and toss to coat.

2. In a bowl, mix lime juice with salt, pepper, oil, vinegar and

stevia and stir well.

3. Add this to salad, toss to coat, sprinkle cilantro and serve.

Nutrition: cal. 100, fat 10, fiber 2, carbs 5, protein 8

45. <u>Avocado And Egg Salad</u>

Preparation time: 10 minutes **Cooking time:** 7 minutes **Servings:** 4

Ingredients:

- 4 cups mixed lettuce leaves, torn
- 4 eggs
- 1 avocado, pitted and sliced
- ¼ cup mayonnaise
- 2 tsp. mustard
- 2 garlic cloves, minced
- 1 tbsp. chives, chopped
- Salt and black pepper to the taste

Instructions:

1. Put water in a pot, add some salt, add eggs, bring to a boil over medium high heat, boil for 7 minutes, drain, cool, peel and chop them.

2. In a salad bowl, mix lettuce with eggs and avocado.

3. Add chives and garlic, some salt and pepper and toss to coat.

4. In a bowl, mix mustard with mayo, salt and pepper and stir well.

5. Add this to salad, toss well and serve right away.

Nutrition: cal. 234, fat 12, fiber 4, carbs 7, protein 12

46. <u>Avocado And Cucumber Salad</u>

Preparation time: 10 minutes **Cooking time:** 0 minutes **Servings:** 4

Ingredients:

- 1 small red onion, sliced
- 1 cucumber, sliced
- 2 avocados, pitted, peeled and chopped
- 1 pound cherry tomatoes, halved

- 2 tbsp. olive oil
- ¼ cup cilantro, chopped
- 2 tbsp. lemon juice
- Salt and black pepper to the taste

Instructions:

1. In a large salad bowl, mix tomatoes with cucumber, onion and avocado and stir.

2. Add oil, salt, pepper and lemon juice and toss to coat well.

3. Serve cold with cilantro on top.

Nutrition: cal.140, fat 4, fiber 2, carbs 4, protein 5

Dessert and Snacks Recipes

47. **Tasty Nutella**

Preparation time: 10 minutes **Cooking time:** 0 minutes **Servings:** 6

Ingredients:

- 2 ounces coconut oil
- 4 tbsp. cocoa powder
- 1 tsp. vanilla extract
- 1 cup walnuts, halved
- 4 tbsp. stevia

Instructions:

1. In your food processor, mix cocoa powder with oil, vanilla, walnuts and stevia and blend very well.

2. Keep in the fridge for a couple of hours and then serve.

Nutrition: cal.100, fat 10, fiber 1, carbs 3, protein 2

48. <u>Mug Cake</u>

Preparation time: 2 minutes **Cooking time:** 3 minutes **Servings:** 1

Ingredients:

- 4 tbsp. almond meal
- 2 tbsp. ghee
- 1 tsp. stevia
- 1 tbsp. cocoa powder, unsweetened

- 1 egg
- 1 tbsp. coconut flour
- ¼ tsp. vanilla extract
- ½ tsp. baking powder

Instructions:

1. Put the ghee in a mug and introduce in the microwave for a couple of seconds.

2. Add cocoa powder, stevia, egg, baking powder, vanilla and coconut flour and stir well.

3. Add almond meal as well, stir again, introduce in the microwave and cook for 2 minutes.

4. Serve your mug cake with berries on top.

Nutrition: cal. 450, fat 34, fiber 7, carbs 10, protein 20

49. Delicious Sweet Buns

Preparation time: 10 minutes **Cooking time:** 30 minutes **Servings:** 8

Ingredients:

- ½ cup coconut flour
- 1/3 cup psyllium husks
- 2 tbsp. swerve
- 1 tsp. baking powder
- A pinch of salt
- ½ tsp. cinnamon
- ½ tsp. cloves, ground
- 4 eggs
- Some chocolate chips, unsweetened
- 1 cup hot water

Instructions:

1. In a bowl, mix flour with psyllium husks, swerve, baking powder, salt, cinnamon, cloves and chocolate chips and stir well.

2. Add water and egg, stir well until you obtain a dough, shape 8 buns and arrange them on a lined baking sheet.

3. Introduce in the oven at 350 degrees and bake for 30 minutes.

4. Serve these buns with some almond milk and

Nutrition: cal. 100, fat 3, fiber 3, carbs 6, protein 6

50. <u>Lemon Custard</u>

Preparation time: 10 minutes **Cooking time:** 30 minutes **Servings:** 6

Ingredients:

- 1 and 1/3 pint almond milk
- 4 tbsp. lemon zest
- 4 eggs
- 5 tbsp. swerve
- 2 tbsp. lemon juice

Instructions:

1. In a bowl, mix eggs with milk and swerve and stir very well.

2. Add lemon zest and lemon juice, whisk well, pour into ramekins and place them into a baking dish with some water on the bottom.

3. Bake in the oven at 360 degrees F for 30 minutes.

4. Leave custard to cool down before serving it.

Nutrition: cal. 120, fat 6, fiber 2, carbs 5, protein 7

51. **Chocolate Ganache**

Preparation time: 1 minute **Cooking time:** 5 minutes **Servings:** 6

Ingredients:

- ½ cup heavy cream
- 4 ounces dark chocolate, unsweetened and chopped

Instructions:

1. Put cream into a pan and heat up over medium heat.

2. Take off heat when it begins to simmer, add chocolate pieces and stir until it melts.

3. Serve this very cold as a dessert or use it as a cream for a keto cake.

Nutrition: cal. 78, fat 1, fiber 1, carbs 2, protein 0

CPSIA information can be obtained
at www.ICGtesting.com
Printed in the USA
BVHW090033280421
605944BV00005B/956

9 781801 882286